All About Animals

What's an AMPHIBIAN?

Anna Kaspar

PowerKiDS press

New York

Published in 2012 by The Rosen Publishing Group, Inc.
29 East 21st Street, New York, NY 10010

First Edition

Editor: Amelie von Zumbusch
Book Design: Ashley Drago

Photo Credits: Cover © www.iStockphoto.com/Wojciech Gajda; pp. 5, 13, 22 Shutterstock.com; pp. 6, 18, 24 (sugarcane) iStockphoto/Thinkstock; p. 9 © www.iStockphoto.com/Mark Kostich; p. 10 © www.iStockphoto.com/Tommounsey; pp. 14–15 © www.iStockphoto.com/Melinda Fawver; p. 17 © www.iStockphoto.com/Yan Gluzberg; p. 21 Paul Oomen/Getty Images.

Library of Congress Cataloging-in-Publication Data

Kaspar, Anna.
 What's an amphibian? / by Anna Kaspar. — 1st ed.
     p. cm. — (All about animals)
 Includes index.
 ISBN 978-1-4488-6138-5 (library binding) — ISBN 978-1-4488-6234-4 (pbk.) — ISBN 978-1-4488-6235-1 (6-pack)
 1. Amphibians—Juvenile literature. I. Title.
 QL644.2.K376 2012
 597.8—dc23
                                   2011020459

Manufactured in the United States of America

CPSIA Compliance Information: Batch #WW12PK: For Further Information contact Rosen Publishing, New York, New York at 1-800-237-9932

Contents

Do you know what kind of animal a frog is? It is an amphibian.

5

Salamanders, newts, and toads are amphibians, too. Most amphibians have wet skin.

Amphibians are cold-blooded. They use the Sun's heat to stay warm.

An amphibian's body changes as it grows. For example, **tadpoles** turn into frogs.

Baby amphibians breathe with **gills**. Older ones may breathe through their skin or lungs.

13

Eastern newts live in North America. Newts become **efts** before they become adults.

American bullfrogs are noisy. They are North America's biggest frogs.

Poison dart frogs come from South America and Central America.

Fire salamanders live in Europe.
They most often live in forests.

22

Cane toads often eat bugs on **sugarcane** crops. This is how they got their name.

WORDS TO KNOW

eft

gills

sugarcane

tadpole

INDEX

WEB SITES

Due to the changing nature of Internet links, PowerKids Press has developed an online list of Web sites related to the subject of this book. This site is updated regularly. Please use this link to access the list:
www.powerkidslinks.com/aaa/amphib/

24